Your Mission Book

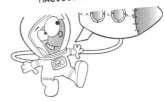

Look Down... Look Up!	2
The **I.D.E.A.S.** Process	4
The **WAGiWays** for Safety	9
Your **Missions**:	10
1. Gravity	10
Let's Build a Contraption	13
2. LiftOff!	19
Let's Build a Bottle Rocket	22
Let's Create Rocket Fuel	25
Mind-Blowing Space Facts	28
3. Life in Space	33
Let's Create a "Space Diaper"	36
4. Return Home	42
Let's Land an Egg	44
Our Team	48

www.wagilabs.org

WAGiLabs is a nonprofit 501 (c)(3) organization.
Copyright 2024 WAGiLabs. All rights reserved.
woof@wagilabs.org • +1 434-296-6138

Look Down.

What do you see?

Your hands, your phone, your shoes, the earth.

These are things within your reach and your control.

Now, Look Up!

What do you see? The ceiling! That's not exciting!

If you're lucky to be outside, you see clouds drifting by, stars twinkling at night, maybe a satellite or the International Space Station orbiting overhead.

Looking up helps us see what's possible and drives us to seek new things. **Looking up** inspires creativity and encourages engineers to explore space and travel to faraway places like the Moon and Mars.

This passion for **science**, **technology**, **engineering** and **math** - or **STEM** - starts with the wonder of looking up! **STEM** education has three key goals:

1. Preparing students for college and careers in cutting-edge STEM fields.

2. Developing skills like logical reasoning, creativity, and collaboration.

3. Making all subjects fun and exciting through hands-on learning.

To understand **STEM**, you need to understand the scientific way of thinking.

STEM involves questioning like a scientist, inventing like a technologist, designing like an engineer, and recognizing patterns like a mathematician.

SCIENCE	TECHNOLOGY	ENGINEERING	MATHEMATICS
Questioning	Inventing	Designing	Patterning
Observing	Using Tools	Creating	Sequencing
Experimenting	Identifying Issues	Building	Numbering
Predicting	Making Stuff Work	Solving	Shaping

The process boils down to five steps you can remember with the acronym **I.D.E.A.S**:

1. Identify the Problem
2. Design a Solution
3. Experiment and Test
4. Analyze the Results
5. Share your Findings

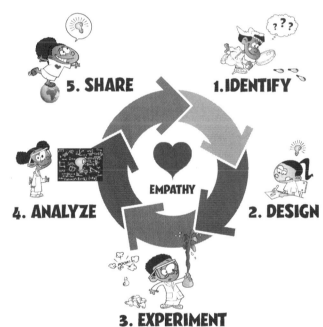

So **look up**, get inspired, and use the **IDEAS** process to help create an amazing future. The whole universe is waiting for you!

The IDEAS Process

Your Guide to Changing the World!

Step One: IDENTIFY the Challenge

Be a detective and ask the five "W" questions (**What**, **Why**, **Who**, **When**, and **Where**) to uncover the problem you want to solve.

1. **WHAT** do people need?

   Ex: In many parts of the world, people lack access to clean drinking water, essential for health and survival.

2. **WHY** is it important to solve this? How will life get better?"

   Ex: Clean water means healthier kids who can attend school regularly.

3. **WHO** is facing the challenge? "Walk in their shoes."

   Ex: People in remote villages have to walk for hours to collect clean water.

4. **WHEN** does the challenge occur?

   Ex: Every single day, and with every sip of contaminated water.

5. **WHERE** does the challenge occur?

   Ex: In developing countries and rural areas without proper infrastructure.

Now you can define your challenge.

What + Why + Who + When + Where =
Your Challenge Definition

Now, turn your answers to the "W" questions into a one sentence definition of your challenge starting with:

"How might we _____?"

For example:

> "How might we ensure that every child, no matter where they live, has access to safe, clean drinking water?"

Once you have the definition of your challenge, you are ready to brainstorm possible solutions.

Step Two: DESIGN a Solution

When we "brainstorm" ideas, we let all our creativity flow like swirling winds in a storm. Brain—Storm, get it? No idea is too big or too small.

Here are your guidelines for brainstorming:

Dream **BIG!**

Say "Yes, **AND**..." to all ideas.

Be **Curious** first... critical second.

Come up with as many ideas as you can.

Build on the ideas of others.

Encourage "**Wild**" even impossible ideas.

Spark your creativity with **What if** ...? questions:

1. **What if** we did _____?
2. **What if** we changed _____?
3. **What if** everyone could _____?
4. **What if** we had _____?
5. **What if** you had all the money in the world?

For example:

What if we could create a low-cost, easy-to-use water purification system?

What if we harnessed the power of the sun to clean water?

What if we could involve the whole community in solving this problem?

Then, record ideas that come from your "**What if** ...?" questions.

Now, identify the **strengths** of each idea.

For each idea, ask the team:

"**Why** is it a **good** idea?"

"**What** is **right** about it"

Finally, think of three ways each idea might help solve your challenge.

_____

_____

_____

Step Three: EXPERIMENT and Test

Turn your ideas into reality by building prototypes you can test.

Some prototypes, such as sketches or storyboards, show your idea. Others, like mock-ups or models, demonstrate how your idea works.

For the water purification example this prototype might be:

- A scale model of a solar-powered water filtration device.
- Sketches showing a community water project.
- An educational game that teaches about the importance of clean water and sanitation.

Step Four: ANALYZE

Put your solutions to the test and see how well they work in real life. Gather feedback from the people you're trying to help. Keep improving your ideas until you've created something that makes a difference.

Step Five: SHARE

Craft an unforgettable pitch that showcases the incredible impact your solution will have. Make people feel the problem's urgency and inspire them to take action.

For example:

> *"No child should have to risk their life every time they drink water. Our innovative solar water purifier will bring clean water to our community, one sip at a time!"*

Mission Action Plan

It's time to introduce the **Mission Action Plan**, we call the **MAP**.

You will fill this out as you progress through the missions and turn the **MAP** into your teacher to get credit for your participation.

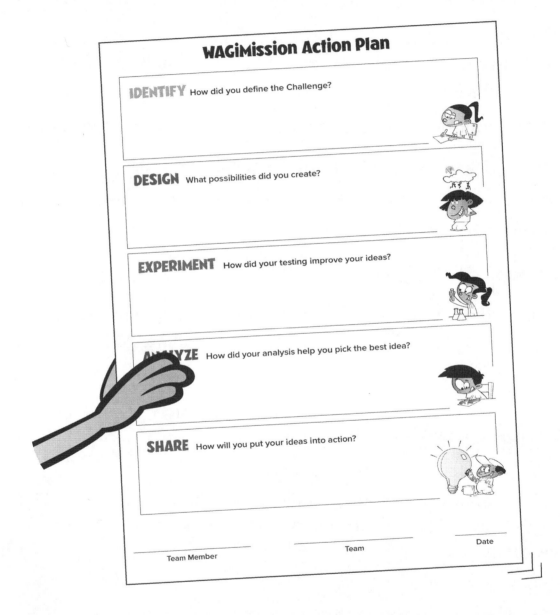

Here's a link to download a copy of the **Mission Action Plan**.

www.wagilabs.org/resources

WAGiWays
for Safety and Collaboration

1. **Create a Safe Space:** We start by being kind to everyone. We use safety gear, such as goggles, gloves, and lab coats. We have a well-equipped first-aid kit and emergency contact information on hand, just in case.

2. **Dream Big:** We brainstorm a lot of amazing ideas!

3. **Yes, AND:** We say: "Yes, **AND**..." when someone shares an idea. It means "I hear your idea **AND** I'm ready to learn more and grow."

4. **Walk-in Others' Shoes:** We imagine what other people's lives are like by "**trying on their shoes**" so we can see the world through their eyes.

5. **Do Good:** We focus on ideas that make life better for our community and the world.

6. **Get Messy:** We experiment and learn through trial and error. We learn how to properly dispose of all materials and clean up our workspace after the experiments.

7. **Keep Going:** We try different solutions when our first attempt doesn't work.

8. **Play It Forward:** We leave footprints that become a pathway to invention for kids around the world.

Gravity

We'll now use the five steps of the **I.D.E.A.S.** process on our first mission: learning about **gravity**.

At WAGiLabs, we were on a kidpreneurship journey of **looking down** and identifying community challenges and then brainstorm solutions to present at the GuppyTank.

Now we are going to **look up** to space and see how our astronauts get there safely, how they live once in space, and how they return home. We'll start our missions by first learning about gravity.

Here on Earth, gravity is a constant force that affects everything we do. We experience gravity whenever we drop something and watch it fall to the ground. Gravity keeps our feet on the planet and holds objects in place, even very heavy ones.

Think about a construction site and how we can lift beams, glass and metal to make buildings soar far into the sky.

Despite the strong pull of gravity, we can construct tall skyscrapers by using simple machines as tools. **Simple machines have few or no moving parts that make work easier.**

What are Simple Machines?

Here are examples of six simple machines:

1. What is a **PULLEY**, and how does it help us?

   A pulley is a wheel with a groove that holds a rope or cable. It helps us lift heavy objects more easily, like when you use a flag pole to raise a flag.

2. What is an **INCLINED PLANE**, and how does it help us?

   An inclined plane is a flat surface higher on one end, like a ramp. It helps us move heavy objects up or down, like rolling a heavy barrel up a ramp into a truck.

3. What is a **LEVER**, and how does it help us?

   A lever is an extended object that pivots on a point, like a see-saw. It helps us lift heavy objects by applying force on one end, like using a crowbar to pry open a box.

4. What are a **WHEEL** and **AXLE**, and how do they help us?

   A wheel and axle consists of a round object (wheel) attached to a rod (axle). They help us move things easily, like on a wagon, car, or bicycle.

5. What is a **WEDGE**, and how does it help us?

   A wedge is an object with one thick end that gets thinner towards the other end, like a doorstop. It helps us split things apart, like using an axe to chop wood.

6. What is a **SCREW**, and how does it help us?
   A screw is an inclined plane wrapped around a cylinder, like a bolt or a jar lid. It helps us hold things together or lift things, like screwing a light bulb into a socket to hold it in place.

Now that you understand simple machines, you are going to design and build a Rube Goldberg-like contraption **to put a marble into a paper cup**.

Rube Goldberg (1883-1970) was a cartoonist, sculptor, engineer, and inventor. Rube created wacky, complicated contraptions that performed simple tasks like opening an umbrella, scratching someone's back, or sharpening a pencil.

A Rube Goldberg contraption consists of a series of simple machines linked together to produce a domino effect, in which each device triggers the next one, and the original goal is achieved only after many steps.

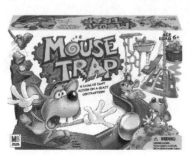

You may be more familiar with his work than you think: If you've played the classic "Mouse Trap" board game, you've experienced the fun of Rube's creations.

Let's Build a Contraption

You are going to design and build a Rube Goldberg-like contraption **to put a marble into a paper cup**.

Your contraption must:

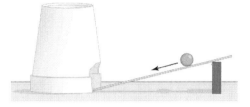

- Include at least **four** different **simple machines**

- Be made with recycled or repurposed materials
- Have at twenty six distinct **steps**
- Tell a story about the challenges you are trying to solve with these simple machines and how this exercise relates to everyday life challenges.

A step is defined as a single action or movement. For example, a marble rolling down an inclined plane would be one step, and putting the marble in the cup is another step.

Why 26 Steps?

Rube Goldberg said most people go from point A to point B in life as quickly as possible.

He wanted to go from A to B, **using all the letters in the alphabet** to see new ideas and experience life. There are 26 letters in the alphabet.

If you create a contraption with 26 steps, please email a video to woof@wagilabs.org, and you'll receive a cool prize and a social media spotlight for your contraption.

Needed Materials:

All teams will need identical marbles and paper cups. You can use any additional materials you'd like, but please **DO NOT** go out and buy materials. The fun and creativity of a Rube Goldberg contraption comes from the challenge of working with and re-purposing everyday items.

Think about bringing:

- Cardboard
- Toilet paper rolls
- Egg cartons
- Legos
- String

- Clean Food Containers
- Toy Cars
- Duct Tape
- Scissors
- Ruler

You'll also want an adult, like a relative, family friend, or your favorite teacher, to review and judge your contraption using the provided criteria.

Judging Criteria:

These points will be awarded based on the final run, and no points will be awarded on any practice runs.

Number of simple machines used   ____ x 15 points   = ____

Number of different materials used ____ x 15 points   = ____

Number of fixes to complete run   ____ x (-15 points) = ____

The challenge story you tell (up to 25 points)   = ____

                                                          TOTAL ____

Borrow Some Ideas

Here is a link to Rube Goldberg videos on YouTube that might give you some design ideas. It's OK to "borrow" the ideas demonstrated in the videos.

https://www.youtube.com/channel/UCp7FcZAAyqnBunO6eAAh8NQ

Here is a successful contraption for turning on a light.

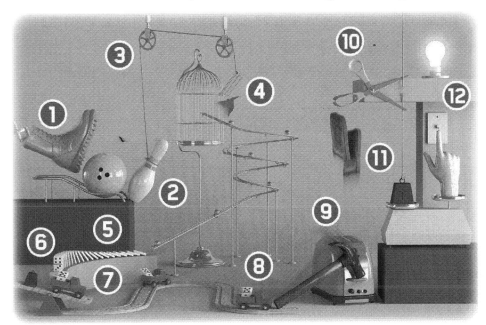

Here are the twelve steps in the light chain reaction:

1. A boot kicks a bowling ball.
2. The bowling ball knocks over a bowling pin.
3. The falling pin pulls a rope to open a birdcage.
4. The escaping bird bumps a ball down a track.
5. The ball knocks over dominoes.
6. A domino falls into a truck.
7. The domino rolls down a seesaw.
8. The domino knocks over a hammer.
9. The falling hammer turns on a toaster.
10. The toast pops up and hits scissors, which cut a rope.
11. A weight falls onto one side of a balance.
12. The hand on the other side of the balance rises, flipping the light switch.

It's Time to Brainstorm:

Your brainstorming goal is to devise creative ways to put the marble in the cup using as many steps as possible.

1. Each team member will work on their own for **20 minutes** and sketch a draft of a contraption and a story for what challenge you are trying to overcome.

2. The first step starts with releasing the marble, and the last step is the marble dropping into a cup.

3. Share your design with your team members.

4. As a team, decide which components you like from each person's design.

5. Combine your best ideas to sketch your team's contraption and the story your team will tell.

Now, It's Time to Build:

1. Start building your contraption.

2. Label each step and simple machine used.

3. Give your turns and twists fun and descriptive names.

4. Celebrate success with sounds, flags, billboards, whatever you can dream up!

5. Do trial runs of the marble through the simple machines.

6. Tweak the machines to allow a flawless run of the marble into the cup.

7. Now, it's time to present your story and do your final run.

It's Time to Present:

1. Every contraption needs to tell a story of overcoming a life challenge. What story does your machine tell?

2. You'll present your story before launching your final run in the competition.

3. Pick who the presenters will be.

4. Practice telling your story and following the story with a demonstration of your contraption.

5. Pick the guides that will help out if your marble gets stuck.

6. Now, **ROLL THE MARBLE!**

It's Time to Journal:

1. What did you learn from this exercise?

2. How did you use STEM in building the contraption?

3. What ideas from this exercise can you apply to other life challenges?

4. Did you experience what engineers call learning from "trial and error?"

Mission Action Plan

Now it's time to fill out the MAP on the next page and turn it into your teacher to get credit for your participation.

WAGiMission Action Plan

IDENTIFY How did you define the Challenge?

DESIGN What possibilities did you create?

EXPERIMENT How did your testing improve your ideas?

ANALYZE How did your analysis help you pick the best idea?

SHARE How will you put your ideas into action?

Team Member   Team   Date

Liftoff!

We are going to build a bottle rocket and blast off **outside**!!! First, we must learn what a rocket is and what physical and chemical reactions allow it to overcome gravity and take off into the sky.

A rocket is a vehicle propelled by one or more engines that launches something into the sky.

In 1232, the Chinese invented **solid fuel** rockets. Solid fuel rockets typically burn a mix of nitrate, carbon, and sulfur — the same ingredients used in gunpowder but mixed in proportions to allow them to burn rapidly without exploding.

Solid-fuel rockets work well for blasting satellites into space, but the engine and thrust cannot be controlled.

So, scientists invented a different rocket that burns **liquid fuel**, such as liquid oxygen and liquid hydrogen. The engines and thrust on these rockets can be controlled, making them ideal for space missions like sending a spacecraft with people in it to the moon!

Examples of rockets you might have heard about:

1. The Saturn V rocket that took astronauts to the moon.
2. The Space Shuttle that carried astronauts and cargo to the International Space Station.
3. SpaceX's Falcon 9 rocket that launches satellites and spacecraft.
4. NASA's powerful new rocket, the Space Launch System (SLS), will help send astronauts to the moon and Mars!

Newton's Third Law of Motion

We need to learn about the Third Law of Motion to understand how a rocket works. This law says, "For every action, there is an equal and opposite reaction." It might sound unclear, but it's like playing a tug-of-war game!

Imagine you're in a swimming pool, pushing off against the wall with your feet. What happens? You go gliding through the water in the opposite direction! That's Newton's Third Law in action. When you push the wall, the wall pushes you back with the same force but in the opposite direction.

A powerful engine in a rocket creates a chemical reaction that makes hot gases come out of the rocket's tail quickly. This vital force pushes the rocket off the launchpad and into the sky.

The power of a rocket is called thrust. It takes a lot of thrust to lift a rocket off the ground and fuel to create that much thrust. One of the biggest challenges in building a rocket is figuring out how to carry enough fuel to complete its mission without being too heavy.

Rockets fly because they can generate a force called lift, which moves the rocket upward. The rocket's forward motion creates lift as it moves through the air. This motion is made possible by the thrust from the engine(s).

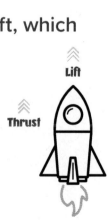

There are four main forces acting on a rocket: Thrust, Lift, Drag, and Weight.

1. **Thrust:** The force that pushes the rocket forward.
2. **Lift:** The force that moves the rocket upward.
3. **Drag:** The force created by air resistance, which tries to slow the rocket down.
4. **Weight:** The force created by gravity pulls the rocket back toward Earth.

When the thrust is greater than the drag, the rocket moves forward. When the lift is greater than the weight, the rocket moves upward.

The size and weight of a rocket depend on what it's carrying into space (called the payload) and how much fuel it needs to lift off.

For example, the Mars Rover Curiosity is about the same size as a car and weighs almost 2,000 pounds! It was launched on a particular rocket with enough fuel to break through Earth's gravity and send Curiosity to Mars.

Rockets are often built in stages, with the first and biggest stage used for lifting off from Earth. Extra stages are used to send the payload to its destination in space.

Let's Build a Bottle Rocket!

Needed Materials:

- A large, empty plastic soda bottle (no larger than 2 liters)
- Cardboard, tape
- A cork that fits the neck of the soda bottle
- A bicycle pump with a needle adapter
- Water
- Markers, paint and tin foil to decorate your rocket.

Time to Brainstorm and Build:

1. The large soda bottle will serve as the body of the rocket.
2. Paint the bottle and use tin foil to create a nose cone or cover the fins.
3. Cut four triangles out of cardboard to make fins 4-inches tall.
4. Use tape to attach fins around the top neck of the bottle, near the cap. You will turn the bottle upside down so the neck of the bottle is at the bottom of the rocket.
5. Create a nose cone out of cardboard for the top.
6. Fill the bottle one-quarter full of water.
7. Make sure the needle on the air pump is longer than the cork. If not, trim the cork so that the needle is longer.
8. Push the cork into the opening of the bottle. It should fit snugly and prevent the water from leaking out.

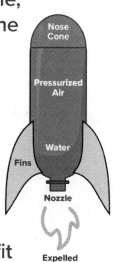

22

Now go outside and find an open space where you can conduct this experiment without risking the well-being of others, animals, or property.

It's time to put on your safety goggles.

1. Connect the bottle to the pump by inserting the needle into the cork.

2. Set it up with the top of the bottle with the cork pointed down at the bottom of the rocket.

3. Please make sure the fins are strong enough to hold it up on its own. If not, modify the fins or create a launch stand.

4. Stand back from your rocket.

5. Carefully pump air into the bottle. The bottle will launch as the air pressure inside the bottle increases.

6. This pressure increase will knock the cork out of the bottle while pushing water out in the downward direction, pushing the bottle skyward.

7. Did your rocket launch? If not, try to figure out why and what you need to change to achieve liftoff. Then try it again.

8. If it did launch, how high did your rocket go? Did it go higher than your house or your tallest tree? Did it reach the clouds?

9. Is there anything else you would change about your rocket design to improve its performance?

WAGiMission Action Plan

IDENTIFY How did you define the Challenge?

DESIGN What possibilities did you create?

EXPERIMENT How did your testing improve your ideas?

ANALYZE How did your analysis help you pick the best idea?

SHARE How will you put your ideas into action?

Team Member   Team   Date

Let's Create "Rocket Fuel!"

Needed Materials:

- Three plastic 16 oz water bottles
- Three balloons
- 3 Tablespoons of baking soda
- 8 ounces of water
- 8 ounces of club soda
- 8 ounces of vinegar
- Measuring cup
- Funnel
- Tape

In this exercise, we will "test" the properties of different combinations of simulated "rocket fuel." This exercise may get messy, so dress appropriately and wear your safety goggles!

1. One experiment will test water and baking soda.
2. The second experiment will test club soda and baking soda.
3. The third will test vinegar and baking soda.

The balloons will contain the baking soda and be attached to the water bottles so that when the two ingredients mix, the balloon captures the gas produced by the chemical reaction.

Instructions:

1. Add one tablespoon of baking soda to each of the balloons with a funnel.

2. Set up three water bottles. Each one will have 8 ounces of liquid. The first will have water, the second will have club soda, and the third will have vinegar. You can write the type of liquid on the outside of the bottle to keep track.

3. Carefully attach one of the balloons to the neck of each bottle. Be sure that you don't add the powder to the liquid. The balloon should fit tightly over the neck of the bottle. You can tape the balloon onto the bottleneck to ensure it stays on during the chemical reaction.

4. When all three bottles are set up, carefully lift the balloons to empty the powder from the balloon into the liquid.

5. Observe the reactions.

6. Can you explain what happened?

7. What happens if you gently shake the liquid in the bottles?

8. Which mixture would you choose to fuel your rocket, and explain why?

Time To Journal:

1. What did you learn from these exercises?

2. How did you use **STEM** in building the fuel and the rocket?

3. What ideas from this exercise can you apply to other challenges?

WAGiMission Action Plan

IDENTIFY — How did you define the Challenge?

DESIGN — What possibilities did you create?

EXPERIMENT — How did your testing improve your ideas?

ANALYZE — How did your analysis help you pick the best idea?

SHARE — How will you put your ideas into action?

Team Member _____ Team _____ Date _____

"Mind-Blowing"
Facts about Outer Space!

First up, did you know that space is **completely silent**? Sound needs two essential things to travel: a medium (like air, water, or solid objects) and vibrations. When you clap your hands or play music, it makes the air around it vibrate. Those vibrations bounce off your eardrums, and your brain interprets them as sound. Pretty cool, right?

Now, here's the thing about space — it's **mostly empty**! There are huge distances between stars and planets, and there's practically nothing in between. It's like a giant cosmic vacuum. And because there's no air or other medium in space for sound to travel through, vibrations can't bounce around like they do here on Earth.

Imagine you're an astronaut floating outside your spacecraft. Even if you scream at the top of your lungs, **no one would hear you** — not even another astronaut right next to you! The sound waves from your voice wouldn't have any air to vibrate so they couldn't reach anyone's ears.

That's why you might hear loud explosions or spaceship noises in movies about space, but those sounds don't exist in space. Filmmakers add them to make the story more exciting, but the space is completely silent.

 Now, let's talk about **Mars**. First, you'll notice that gravity is only about one-third as strong as it is on Earth. This means you'd feel much lighter, and every step would be bouncy.

You could **jump three times higher** than you can on Earth, and it would take longer to fall back down. It would be like having superpowers! You could jump so high that dunking a basketball would be a piece of cake. Mars is a slam dunk!

 Let's take a trip to **Venus**. Venus is the hottest planet in our solar system, with surface temperatures reaching a scorching 900°F (480°C). That's **hot enough to melt lead!** Your spacesuit must be incredibly well-insulated to protect you from the searing heat.

Imagine a giant cosmic bathtub filled with water. If you could put all the planets in our solar system into this tub, most would sink straight to the bottom. But **Saturn** would be the one planet that would **float on top of the water** like a rubber ducky!

That's because Saturn is less dense than water — about 30% less dense. It's because of what Saturn is made of. While it does have a small, rocky core, most of Saturn is made up of swirling gas and liquid, mainly hydrogen and helium. Gas is much less dense than rock or liquid, so Saturn's overall density is lower Earth's.

Now, let's talk about **wind**. The wind is just air that's moving from one place to another. On Earth, we feel the wind when we step outside on a breezy day or see leaves rustling in the trees. Sometimes, when the wind is mighty, like during a hurricane or a tornado, it can even be strong enough to pick up cars and houses!

 But the winds on Earth are nothing compared to the winds on **Neptune**. On this giant, blue, gas-giant planet, wind speeds can reach an incredible 1,600 miles per hour (2,575 kilometers per hour)! That's like zooming from one end of the United States to the other in just one hour!

In perspective, the strongest winds ever recorded on Earth were during Typhoon Tip in 1979, reaching 190 miles per hour (306 kilometers per hour). That's still really fast, but it's only about one-eighth the speed of Neptune's cosmic hurricanes!

Did you know that astronauts' **footprints on the moon can stay there for 100 million years** or more? That's because the moon doesn't have wind, rain, or weather like we do on Earth, so there's nothing to wash away or cover up the footprints.

When an astronaut steps on the moon, their heavy boots sink about an inch (2.5 centimeters) into the soft, dusty surface, creating a footprint that stays put. The only way the footprints could be erased is if another astronaut or a moon rover drives over them.

Did you know there's a planet called **HD 189733b**, about 63 lightyears from Earth, where it **rains glass**? The wind on this planet is so strong that it blows the glass sideways, making it look like a never-ending glass storm.

The planet is incredibly hot, reaching over 1,800 degrees Fahrenheit (1,000 degrees Celsius) – hot enough to melt sand into glass! The planet also has winds that blow up to 5,400 miles per hour (8,700 kilometers per hour), more than six times faster than the strongest winds on Earth. These winds can blow the glass rain sideways, creating a never-ending storm of sharp, shiny shards.

Let's imagine that you have a twin, and while you live on Earth, your twin lives on **Venus**. Now, here's where things get interesting – if you could magically see each other, you'd notice something strange: **your twin on Venus would be aging faster than you!**

You might be wondering how this is possible. Well, it all has to do with something called time dilation. Time doesn't always move at the same speed everywhere in the universe.

On Earth, we're used to time ticking away at a steady pace, but on other planets, like Venus, time can move slower or faster. In the case of Venus, time moves slower than it does on Earth. This means that if you and your twin were born simultaneously, your twin on Venus would be aging faster than you.

So, while you might be celebrating your 10th birthday on Earth, your twin on Venus could already be a teenager!

Deep out in space, there's an asteroid called "**29132 Bradmohney**." But here's the funny thing – this asteroid isn't shaped like an ordinary rock. Instead, it's shaped like a rectangle, just like SpongeBob himself!

The asteroid was discovered by a scientist named Brad Mohney, which is why it has "Bradmohney" in its name. But the scientists who found it thought it would be fun to name it after SpongeBob since it has such a unique shape. So, even though SpongeBob lives in a pineapple under the sea, he now has a unique space rock named after him, too!

Light is the quickest thing in the universe, zooming along at an astonishing 186,282 miles per second (299,792 kilometers per second).

To put that in perspective, consider how long it takes you to run around your school or neighborhood. If you could travel at the speed of light, **you could run around the Earth multiple times before you could even finish saying, "Ready, set, go!"**

Now, humans can't travel at the speed of light (at least not yet!), but it's still fun to imagine the incredible adventures we could have if we could. The world would look very different at the speed of light - colors would blur together, and you might even see things happening in reverse!

Plus, you could visit distant planets and stars in the blink of an eye and return home for dinner. So, keep dreaming big and imagining the impossible because who knows? Maybe someday, you'll be the one to unlock the secrets of the universe and take us on lightspeed adventures beyond our wildest dreams!

The future of space exploration is in your hands, and we can't wait to see where your curiosity will take you!

Life In Space

Right now, there could be as many as nine people living and working on the International Space Station, also known as ISS. These astronauts and cosmonauts live in zero gravity, and such a very different setting can disrupt an astronaut's health.

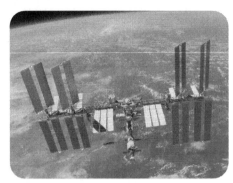

Living in zero gravity can feel like having a constant head cold because the fluids in your body rise to your head, and moving around in zero gravity can cause you to experience motion sickness.

While our day on earth is 24 hours long with one sunrise and one sunset, the ISS orbits the Earth 16 times daily. That makes for a **sunrise every 90 minutes**.

To keep the crew comfortable, the ISS has a galley, refrigerator, freezer, kitchen table, exercise equipment, sleeping cabin, toilet, and washbasin.

When it is time to sleep, astronauts have sleeping bags attached to the wall

of their small crew cabins. They can sleep just about anywhere in the ISS as long as they connect their sleeping bags to something while they are sleeping. They typically sleep for eight hours after a 16-hour mission day, and to block out the light and noise, they may wear sleep masks and earplugs.

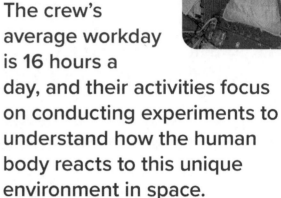

The crew's average workday is 16 hours a day, and their activities focus on conducting experiments to understand how the human body reacts to this unique environment in space.

Maintaining the station is a full-time job in itself. The crew is continuously checking the station systems, cleaning air filters, maintaining equipment, and updating computer equipment to keep it in good condition. The crew must be ready for emergency repairs, spacewalks, and trash duty!

The crew practices daily hygiene, much like they would living on earth. To conserve water, they take sponge baths daily using washcloths and a rinse-less shampoo to wash their hair.

Any excess water has to be captured with a vacuum and suctioned into a tank so it can be recycled and reused the next day. This vacuum also prevents any water from escaping and floating around in space.

The next time you wash your hands or take a shower, think about how lucky we are living on earth with so many water resources and how gravity is working for you.

And just because we know you're wondering: **using the bathroom without gravity is a different experience.**

The toilet aboard the ISS doesn't require flushing because it has fans that suck air and urine through a funnel, a hose, and then into the wastewater tank.

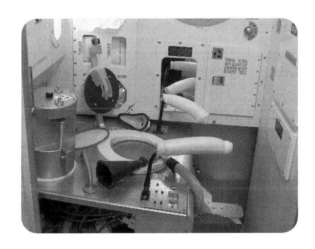

The toilet consists of a toilet bowl and a urine funnel. The astronauts position themselves on the toilet seat using leg restraints and thigh bars. Remember, they are weightless in space and need to use the restraints **so they don't float away.**

The toilet works like a vacuum cleaner with fans that suck air and waste into the commode. Each astronaut has a personal urinal funnel, which has to be attached to the hose's adapter. Fans use air sucked into containers to capture solid waste products and pull the urine through the funnel and hose into the wastewater tank — **no flushing needed.**

Let's Create a Space Diaper!

Managing fluids in space come with a load of unique problems. So NASA developed a "Maximum Absorbency Garment" (MAG) for the shuttle program. They're sometimes called "space diapers."

MAGs are more like hyper-absorbent bike shorts. Several thin layers of material move urine quickly away from the body. Then sodium polyacrylate, a super-absorbent polymer (SAP) crystal material capable of taking on 400 times its weight in water, locks away the moisture.

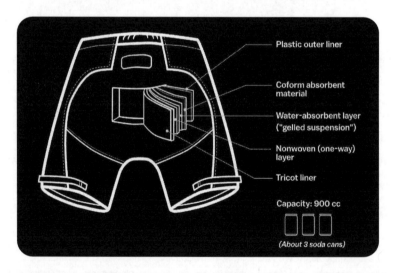

A MAG can soak up 2 liters — or 2.1 quarts — of liquid. That's like absorbing all the liquid in 3 cans of soda!

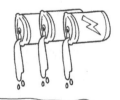

Time to Brainstorm:

Can you think of five more uses for these super-absorbent polymer crystals besides NASA space diapers?

Your Mission:

To experiment with different materials to determine their absorbency properties.

1. Are polycarbonate crystals the best absorber?

2. Rank all of the materials by best absorbency.

3. Rank all of the materials by cost.

4. What materials offer the best value based on the absorption and the cost?

Needed Materials:

1. 10 small cups

2. Different absorbent materials:
   - Polycarbonate crystals
   - Cotton balls
   - Polyester stuffing
   - Clay powder
   - Paper towels
   - Sponges
   - Baking soda
   - Slica gel
   - Activated carbon
   - Cut up washcloths

3. Water and a water dropper

4. Notebook and pencil

Time to Build:

1. Set up each material in a single cup and count how many drops of water are absorbed by the material.

    - Polycarbonate crystals   _____
    - Cotton balls   _____
    - Polyester stuffing   _____
    - Clay powder   _____
    - Paper towels   _____
    - Sponges   _____
    - Baking soda   _____
    - Silica gel   _____
    - Activated carbon   _____
    - Cut up washcloths   _____

2. Which material absorbed the most water drops?

3. Which material absorbed the least amount of water?

4. Which materials absorbed the liquid as you thought?

5. What other materials can you think of to absorb liquids?

6. Sketch your own "Maximum Absorbency Garment." It can be for any use you can think of and include your favorite absorbent materials.

7. What if you created a prototype of the MAG you designed?

- How would you test your design?
- Would you try it on?
- How would you test it to see if it works?

When you test it out, you'll learn some essential information you can use to modify and improve your design.

Time to Present:

Share your new, breakthrough "Maximum Absorbency Garment" with your classmates and tell them about its super absorption capabilities and comfortable design.

Listen to their feedback and make revisions to your design. Then present it to your family and friends. Look for more feedback to improve your design.

Time to Journal:

1. What did you learn from these exercises?
2. How did you use **STEM** in creating your MAG?
3. What ideas from this exercise can you apply to other life challenges?

WAGiMission Action Plan

IDENTIFY — How did you define the Challenge?

DESIGN — What possibilities did you create?

EXPERIMENT — How did your testing improve your ideas?

ANALYZE — How did your analysis help you pick the best idea?

SHARE — How will you put your ideas into action?

_____ _____ _____
Team Member   Team   Date

Fourth Mission

Return Home

Returning to earth might seem like it should be the easiest part of the mission, but it's one of the most challenging!

The Orion spacecraft designed for human exploration has to re-enter the earth's atmosphere traveling at speeds expected to exceed 20,000 mph. While the earth's atmosphere will initially slow the spacecraft down to 325 mph, a unique parachute system is deployed to achieve a safe landing speed of 20 mph or less.

Since the earth is continuously spinning, as soon as the spaceship hits the earth's atmosphere, air particles create friction. This friction helps slow the spacecraft down and causes intense heat during the initial re-entry phase of the landing.

In addition to carrying astronauts, the spacecraft has many delicate sensors and instruments that collect essential data and need to be kept safe from the extreme pressure and heat of landing.

NASA has used multiple ways to slow down and soften the landing of their spacecraft, from balloons to parachutes.

Check out these resources on other spacecraft landings:

https://mars.jpl.nasa.gov/mer/mission/overview/

https://video.nationalgeographic.com/video/news/00000144-0a21-d3cb-a96c-7b2d0bb60000

https://www.youtube.com/watch?v=tdmZAvwznOU

Take a parachute, for example. It allows humans to land safely by decreasing what's known as their terminal velocity. Gravity makes a person accelerate quickly at first when a human is free-falling. However, as air resistance builds up, eventually, the two forces equalize until the human falls at a constant speed. This continuous speed, known as terminal velocity, is still too dangerous for humans to land safely.

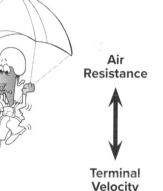

By employing a parachute (which dramatically increases air resistance), the human can then decrease their rate of descent to a safe speed, where they can land on their feet.

Time to Brainstorm:

Which materials would make an excellent parachute, and why?

1.

2.

3.

Which materials would not work for this experiment, and why?

1.

2.

3.

Let's Land an Egg!
Without Breaking It!

You are to build a container that will prevent a raw egg from breaking when dropped from a height of at least 9 feet. Your design will hopefully:

1. Reduce the final speed of the egg by using air resistance.
2. Increase the time of impact by using cushioning.

Needed Materials:

Each group of students gets the following:

- 2 balloons
- 2 small paper cups
- 4 straws
- 1 sq. ft. of plastic wrap
- 1 sq. ft. of aluminum foil
- 4 rubber bands
- 4 popsicle sticks
- 2 ft. of tape
- 1 egg
- 1 bull's eye floor target
- 1 floor covering (newspaper, tarp)
- 1 pair of scissors

Guidelines:

1. If your egg breaks, **it will be a mess.** All teams are responsible for cleaning up after themselves!

2. Your container must be designed so the egg can be inserted easily before competing and quickly checked after the drop.

3. The egg must stay inside the structure throughout the drop.

4. The judges will provide the final competition egg at the time of the competition. It will be a grade A raw egg.

5. There can be no manipulation of the egg to strengthen it.

Scoring Criteria:

1. All unbroken eggs beat all cracked or broken eggs.

2. All cracked eggs beat all broken eggs.

3. If the egg survives the first drop without breaking, the container can be dropped a second time to score more points.

4. If it survives the second drop without breaking, it can be dropped a third time.

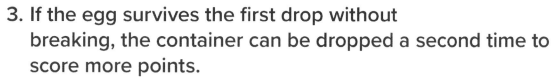

The least materials used in building your structure get **10 bonus points** for every drop.

First Drop:

Hits the bull's eye	10 egg points
Egg is unbroken and not cracked	10 egg points
Egg shell is only cracked	5 egg points
Egg is broken	-10 egg points
Container with least materials used	10 egg points

Second Drop:

Hits the bull's eye	10 egg points
Egg is unbroken and not cracked	10 egg points
Egg shell is only cracked	5 egg points
Egg is broken	-10 egg points
Container with least materials used	10 egg points

Third Drop:

Hits the bull's eye	10 egg points
Egg is unbroken and not cracked	10 egg points
Egg shell is only cracked	5 egg points
Egg is broken	-10 egg points
Container with least materials used	10 egg points

Total Egg Points Score: _____

Time to Journal:

How did you use **STEM** in safely landing your egg?

WAGiMission Action Plan

IDENTIFY — How did you define the Challenge?

DESIGN — What possibilities did you create?

EXPERIMENT — How did your testing improve your ideas?

ANALYZE — How did your analysis help you pick the best idea?

SHARE — How will you put your ideas into action?

_____ _____ _____
Team Member   Team   Date

Our Team

Kathy Schubert

Kathy is the deputy director of the Space Flight Systems Directorate at NASA's Glenn Research Center in Cleveland. Kathy shares the leadership responsibility for space flight and technology development projects and programs, including space propulsion, space power, space communications, microgravity sciences, and materials development programs.

Chic Thompson

Chic is a fellow at the University of Virginia's Darden Business School and adjunct faculty at the Brookings Institution. In 2001, Harvard Business School released a case study on the speaking career of Chic entitled "What a Great Idea!." Chic's first book, "What a Great Idea!," published by HarperCollins was a main selection of the Executive Book Club. His second book, "Yes, But..." is a guide to overcoming the bureaucratic language that stifles continuous innovation. Chic worked in new product development and marketing for W.L. Gore and Associates (Gore-Tex®), Johnson & Johnson, and Walt Disney.

Now, it's YOUR turn to go into Space!

To get there, be curious and keep exploring new ideas. Learn all you can by taking **STEM** classes in Science, Technology, Engineering, and Mathematics.

Made in the USA
Columbia, SC
02 October 2024